America's Game
Oakland Athletics

Paul Joseph

ABDO & Daughters
PUBLISHING

Published by Abdo & Daughters, 4940 Viking Dr., Suite 622, Edina, MN 55435.

Cover photo: Allsport
Interior photos: Wide World Photo, pages 1, 8, 11, 15, 16, 20, 25, 26
                 Allsport, pages 5, 17, 23

Edited by Kal Gronvall

Library of Congress Cataloging–in–Publication Data

Joseph, Paul, 1970-
    Oakland Athletics / Paul Joseph
        p. cm. — (America's game)
    Includes index.
    Summary: Focuses on key players and events in the history of the Oakland Athletics, a team that has played on the East Coast, the West Coast, and in the middle of the country.
    ISBN 1-56239-668-4
    1. Oakland Athletics (Baseball team)—History—Juvenile literature. [1. Oakland Athletics (Baseball team) 2. Baseball—History.] I. Title. II. Series.
GV875.O24J67 1997
796.357'64'0979466—dc20   96-22381
                                                    CIP
                                                    AC

Contents

Oakland Athletics

Since the Oakland Athletics formed in 1901 as part of the original American League (AL), they have played on the East Coast, the West Coast, and had a quick stop in the middle.

The Athletics have been World Champions 9 times, and AL Champions 15 times. They have also finished dead last 25 times.

The franchise has had many outstanding players. Many have been, or will be, inducted into the Baseball Hall of Fame. There have been A's players that hold records that will probably never be broken. The A's have also had players on the field that didn't quite measure up to the standards of a major leaguer.

Through most of the colorful history of the Oakland Athletics there have been two men who really stand out. These two men were indeed opposites. They both had their ups and downs, and their highs and lows. They made the team flourish and they made the team flounder.

One man did it because he loved the game of baseball, and will be remembered forever in a very good light. For the first 50 years of the A's existence the team was managed and partly owned by Connie Mack. Mack was one of the most respected and dignified people in the game of baseball.

Facing page: Athletics' ace base stealer, Rickey Henderson.

4

The other man was Charles O. Finley, a man who was just the opposite of Connie Mack. He ran the team his way after he took over ownership in 1960. Finley was one of the most disliked people in the history of the game. Finley was in it for himself—never taking into consideration the game, the players, or the fans.

Both men won championships and both men suffered miserably with terrible teams. Both had good teams and both had such bad teams that they had trouble filling the stands.

The Athletics' fans look at their history in terms of eras—the Mack era, and the Finley era. And to say that those two eras were both roller coaster rides would be an understatement.

The Philadelphia Athletics

In the late 1800s, the National League (NL) was the dominant professional baseball league. Other leagues would try to compete, but it would never work. Baseball fans would still watch the NL.

Byron Bancroft Johnson wanted to change this. He was determined to come up with a league that would be as popular as the National League. In 1901 it happened—the American League officially began play with eight teams.

Johnson began putting teams in cities where the NL didn't have any—Detroit, Cleveland, and Washington, D.C., for example. He also took a chance and put some teams in cities where there was already an NL team. One of those cities was Philadelphia.

Philadelphia was a great major league town, home of the NL's Phillies. But now they had competition with the new American League team, the Philadelphia Athletics.

The fans and management of the Phillies were very nervous because of their crosstown rival. The Athletics began to lure top players away from the Phillies. The man responsible for starting the Athletics, getting players, getting fans, and keeping it going, was the legendary Connie Mack.

Cornelius Alexander McGilicuddy

Cornelius Alexander McGilicuddy started his career as a player in professional baseball in 1884. As a young, skinny catcher he got the nickname Connie Mack—because that name fit in the box scores in the newspaper. That name stuck, and he was called Connie Mack for the rest of his life.

Connie Mack played in the National League for the Washington Statesmen and for the Pittsburgh Pirates. After managing the Pirates, he decided to take a job with a new team in the American League in 1900, the Philadelphia Athletics.

In 1901, the Athletics had their first season. Mack assembled some great talent by plucking them from the NL. The team finished fourth its first year. In the second year the Athletics moved up and won the American League pennant with 83 victories. (The World Series had not yet been established.)

In 1905, they again won the AL with 92 wins. This time they got their World Series opportunity, taking on the New York Giants. The stronger NL team was too much for the Athletics, taking the World Series in five games.

Facing page: Connie Mack in the Athletics' dugout during a game in 1927.

The First Dynasty

The team was up and down until 1910, when Mack put together one of the best lineups baseball had ever seen. The team included future Hall-of-Famers Eddie Collins, Frank "Home Run" Baker, and Stan Coveleski, all of whom could hit and play solid defense.

Albert Bender and Jack Combs were the star pitchers for the Athletics. Together they combined for a 54-14 record, leading the team to 104 victories. This team was too good for either league, as they ran away with the American League and the World Series, beating the NL Champion Chicago Cubs in five games.

It was Connie Mack's first World Series, but it wouldn't be his last. Again in 1911 and 1913, they won the World Series, beating the Giants both years. In 1914, they again were tops among the AL, but lost in the World Series to the Boston Braves.

Connie Mack and his talented crew established themselves as the first American League dynasty by winning four AL pennants and three World Series titles in those five years.

The bottom began to fall out, however, in 1915. Mack had sold, traded, or lost all of his talent to retirement. Between 1915 and 1921, the team finished in last place each season.

Connie Mack never gave up. He was determined to rebuild his team. And rebuild he did. By 1929, the Athletics had their second dynasty.

Connie Mack (center) with star catcher Mickey Cochrane (left) and pitcher Robert "Lefty" Grove (right).

Lefty Grove

Connie Mack again lured big stars to his team, but this time he had to spend a lot of money to do it. Mickey Cochrane was a future Hall-of-Fame catcher. They acquired a talented young slugger to play first base named James Emory Foxx. Al Simmons was the big hitter for the team, hitting better than .350 and driving in more than 100 runs each of his seasons with the A's.

Mack added a superstar pitcher to round out the lineup. Lefty Grove was purchased for a whopping $100,600 from Baltimore, which was an unheard of sum in those days. Grove quickly led the Athletics to the top of the American League. He was tops in strikeouts every year he pitched for the Athletics.

Grove and the Athletics won the American League Pennant in 1929, 1930, and 1931. They knocked off the great AL New York Yankees, who were led by Babe Ruth and Lou Gehrig, each year.

The 1929 A's won 104 games behind solid pitching and lethal hitting. They cruised to an AL pennant—a staggering 18 games ahead of the Yankees—and advanced to the World Series to meet the Chicago Cubs.

Everyone thought that star pitcher Lefty Grove would start the first World Series game. In a move that startled everyone, Mack started Howard Ehmke—who had only pitched 55 innings all season.

What people didn't know was that Mack had Ehmke scouting the Cubs for the last two weeks of the season. Ehmke studied each player on the Cubs and knew what types of pitches they liked and didn't like.

Ehmke was so good, so well rested, and did his homework to perfection that he made great Cubs' hitters like Rogers Hornsby, Hack Wilson, and Charlie Grimm look silly. Ehmke struck out 13 batters, a World Series record at that time, and led the A's to a 3-1 victory.

Thanks to the great coaching of Connie Mack, the A's easily toppled the stunned Cubs in five games for the World Series title.

Last Hurrah

Mack and the A's were determined to repeat in 1930, and repeat they did. The A's finished the season with 102 victories behind the ace pitching of Grove, who led the league with a 28-5 record. After winning the AL crown, they met the St. Louis Cardinals in a hard-fought series. With great pitching and powerful hitting, the A's prevailed in six games and were World Champs again, much to Connie Mack's delight.

In 1931, the A's won a franchise record 107 games—a record that still stands today—easily making it to the World Series. The A's again would run into the St. Louis Cardinals. The Cardinals wanted revenge from the season before. After a seven-game, down-to-the-wire World Series, they got their revenge. The best team in Athletics' history would come up short and lose the Series to the Cards.

In 1932, the team began to sink. Part of the problem was money. Mack and his team had spent so much money to get great talent that they had nothing left. Attendance began to fall and Mack was forced to break up his second dynasty.

For Mack it was his last dynasty and his last winner. The A's finished in second place in 1932, and third place in 1933. From 1935 to 1950, the best the team finished was fourth place, landing in the cellar 10 times.

In 1950, Connie Mack coached his 50th and final year at the age of 88. Although the team finished in last place, Mack will be remembered for his nine pennants, five World Series titles, his two dynasties, and his all-around love for the game.

Connie Mack died at the age of 94, ending one of the greatest eras baseball had ever witnessed. If you remember baseball, you will remember the man who wore a suit in the dugout—Cornelius Alexander McGilicuddy.

A Quick Stop In The Middle

Businessman Arnold Johnson bought the Athletics from Mack, and found himself with a terrible franchise. In 1954, the team was in last place, 60 games out of first. As a result of their poor record fans stopped coming to the games—the team only drew 304,000 people that year.

Johnson knew something had to be done. He could no longer compete with the mighty NL Philadelphia Phillies. So in 1955, the team moved to Kansas City.

The change of scenery didn't help them win games. Kansas City supported their new team—in the beginning—but after the franchise lost over 100 games four times, they stopped coming, too. Johnson was losing so much money that he finally decided to sell. Charles O. Finley took over full ownership in 1961.

Finley took total control of the Athletics, all the way from the front office to the playing field. Finley did some real strange things. For example, at his home in Chicago, he would listen to the games on the radio and then telephone his instructions to the manager at the game site. Of course, managers didn't like this at all. In Finley's first eight years as owner, he went through seven different managers.

Finley also came up with some outlandish ideas—never before seen in baseball. Among these were a mechanical rabbit that popped out of the turf with fresh baseballs; pink fluorescent lights to mark the foul lines; and a mascot named Charlie O., the mule. He also got

Athletics' owner Charles Finley with team mascot "Charlie O."

rid of the traditional white and blue Athletics' uniforms in favor of green and bright gold ones. Fans were shocked by the new colors.

In the meantime, the team was still losing. But Finley had scouts working hard to find young talent. One by one, Finley signed these future stars, such as Reggie Jackson, Sal Bando, Jim "Catfish" Hunter, Bert Campaneris, and Vida Blue. These players never helped the team in Kansas City, but they would turn the Oakland Athletics into World Champions.

Jim "Catfish" Hunter shows off his pitching style.

Let's Try The West Coast

After 54 years on the east side of the country, and a quick stop in the middle, the Athletics' franchise went to the west coast. With a promise of more money and better fan support, Finley moved his team to California in 1968, and it became the Oakland Athletics. Right out of the gate, the Oakland Athletics began winning, and baseball fans everywhere began to notice them. On May 8, 1968, "Catfish" Hunter pitched a perfect game, a feat that had not been accomplished since 1922!

The A's finished their first season with 82 wins, the most for the franchise in 20 years. Solid pitching and a good offense, led by Reggie Jackson, who finished with 29 home runs, was the key to rebuilding the team. In 1969, Major League Baseball split into two divisions in each league. The Athletics now played in the American League West. Jackson belted 47 home runs in that first season in the AL West. The team followed his lead and began to improve.

By 1971, this young team won 101 games and finished first in the American League West. The key to their success was the pitching of Catfish Hunter, reliever Rollie Fingers, and Vida Blue, who was the AL Most Valuable Player (MVP) and the Cy Young Award winner.

In the American League Championship Series (ALCS), the A's met the Baltimore Orioles—who had a great pitching staff of their own. The Orioles manhandled the A's in three quick games.

This was just the beginning for the A's, who would come back the following year and begin their third dynasty. The team would finally reach the World Series for the first time in 41 years.

Reggie Jackson watches a ball sail into the bleachers.

Oakland

In 1900, baseball legend Connie Mack became the first manager of the Athletics.

Pitcher Robert "Lefty" Grove was tops in strikeouts every year he played with the Athletics.

Reggie Jackson hit 47 home runs for the Athletics in the team's first season in the AL West.

Jim "Catfish" Hunter pitched a perfect game for the Athletics on May 8, 1968.

Athletics

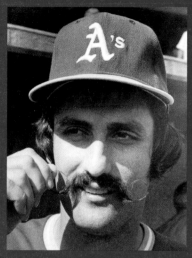

In 1982, Rickey Henderson broke the all-time record for stolen bases with 130.

In 1973, relief pitcher Rollie Fingers racked up 22 saves.

1986 AL Rookie-of-the-Year Jose Canseco finished the season with 33 home runs and 117 RBIs.

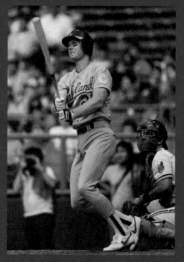

In his rookie season in 1987, Mark McGwire belted 49 home runs, a team record.

An Angry A's Dynasty

In 1972 the young Athletics were the talk of the baseball world. After a terrific 1971 season, everyone predicted them to be the World Champions that year. But there were many problems with the team, mostly because of owner Charles O. Finley. Many players wanted more money after having excellent seasons. But Finley wouldn't budge. The team also was filled with so many egos that it was rare when a week went by without a fight breaking out in the clubhouse.

The team earned the nickname, "The Angry A's," but they all had two things in common: they truly disliked their owner, and they had a burning desire to win. Finley was getting tired of their whining about money, and offered bonuses to any player who grew a mustache. As a result, the team was filled with facial hair, especially Rollie Fingers. Rollie grew a wild, handlebar mustache that he wore the rest of his career.

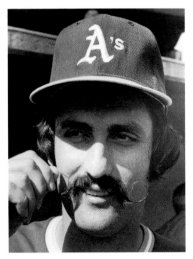

Athletics' relief pitcher Rollie Fingers shows off his handlebar mustache.

But because of their desire to win, the players never let anything get in the way of their ultimate goal. They again captured the American League West, and this time took the ALCS in a tight, five-game series over the Detroit Tigers.

In the World Series, the Athletics had to face the "Big Red Machine" from Cincinnati, who had formidable talent of their own. But it didn't matter. The A's desire to win prevailed over the Reds, and Oakland won the 1972 World Series. They were World Champions for the first time in 42 years.

In 1973, the team continued to win and looked great on the field. But off the field they continued to fight and grumble about Finley. With all of the problems they had, they still managed to win the AL West behind the pitching of Ken Holtzman, Hunter, and Blue, who were all 20-game winners. Fingers added 22 saves.

The A's easily advanced to the World Series and won their second World Championship in a row—but not without controversy. In Game 2, A's second basemen Mike Andrews made two errors that cost the A's the game. Finley was so mad that he wanted to suspend Andrews. But when he couldn't suspend him, he tried to put him on the disabled list. Again he couldn't.

Finally he forced Manager Dick Williams to bench Andrews for the rest of the Series. Immediately following the last game, Dick Williams resigned on national television—after winning two straight championships. Williams could no longer stomach Charlie Finley.

Finley didn't miss a beat. He quickly hired a new manager and the "Angry A's" continued to win.

Behind Cy Young Award-winner Catfish Hunter, and the powerful hitting of Reggie Jackson, the team captured their fourth-straight AL West crown, their third-straight AL crown, and were headed to the World Series for the third time in as many years.

Farewell Charlie O.

The 1974 World Series featured the first-ever all-California match-up, putting the A's against the Los Angeles Dodgers. The A's became only the second franchise in the history of Major League Baseball to win three World Series in a row.

However, that would be it for the Oakland Athletics. The "Angry A's" dynasty was coming to a close. Catfish Hunter headed for the Yankees in 1975. The A's won one more AL West crown, but ended their domination of baseball against the Boston Red Sox in the ALCS. After that they began to fall. Nobody wanted to play for Finley anymore, and Finley didn't want to pay their high salaries. All the talent and the big stars headed to other teams for more money.

The dynasty was over, and the Athletics began to lose many games. By 1979, they fell to last place in the AL West. In 1980, Charles O. Finley's reign was also over for good. He sold the team to California businessman Walter Haas.

When Finley left the team it was in bad shape. He had reduced the front office to six people, and had closed the advertising and promotion department. And the Oakland farm system had next to nothing left in it. Haas would have to start from scratch.

People can say what they want about Finley—which is usually bad—but he did manage to turn a terrible franchise into a three-time World Champion. He may not be remembered in the same light as Connie Mack—but he did leave his mark on Major League Baseball.

Ricky Henderson
steals another base.

The Thief

Although the Athletics were not winning, the fans did have something to cheer about. Rickey Henderson joined the team from the minors in 1979, and quickly established himself as a base-stealing threat. In 1980 "the Thief" stole 100 bases and ran away with the AL record for the most steals in a year.

In the next 11 years, Henderson went on to win the stolen bases title 10 times in the AL. And in 1982, he broke the all-time record—set by Lou Brock—of 118, with an unheard of 130 stolen bases.

Henderson even had the team winning. In the strike-shortened 1981 season the A's managed to win the AL West, but were knocked out by the Yankees in the ALCS.

It wasn't until 1986 when they truly began building for another championship.

Rookies Of The Year

With Rickey Henderson off to the Yankees in 1985, it didn't look good for the Athletics. Then in 1986 came a rookie sensation named Jose Canseco. He finished the season an All-Star, with 33 home runs and 117 RBIs, and the AL Rookie of the Year Award.

In 1987, another rookie sensation came aboard and showed up Canseco. Mark McGwire belted 49 home runs—a team record—in his first year! He too was named Rookie of the Year.

In 1988, the A's added one more AL Rookie of the Year, shortstop Walt Weiss. The bigger news, though, was the pitching. The A's had a staff that led them back to the World Series. Bob Welch, Dave Stewart, Storm Davis, and Todd Burns were the starters, and Dennis Eckersley came on in relief.

The A's put on an awesome display on the way to the World Series in 1988, winning 104 games, and easily winning the AL West behind solid pitching and Jose Canseco's hitting.

Canseco made baseball history, becoming the first player to hit 40 home runs and steal 40 bases. He finished the season with a .307 batting average, 124 RBIs, 42 home runs, and 40 stolen bases.

The A's easily swept Boston in the ALCS. In the World Series they came up short, losing to the underdog Dodgers in five games.

With all the talent coming back in 1989, plus Rickey Henderson re-signing with the team after a few years with the Yanks, the Athletics wouldn't be happy if they didn't get back to the World Series the next year.

Earth-Shaking Champions

The best team in baseball made it back to the World Series. The A's won the American League West behind excellent pitching by Dave Stewart, who had 20 wins, and Davis and Welch, who each had more than 16 wins.

In the ALCS, the A's ran into the talented Toronto Blue Jays. The Jays and A's were evenly matched except for one man: Rickey Henderson.

Oakland won the ALCS in five games. Henderson led both teams in total bases (15), runs (8), RBIs (5), walks (7), on-base percentage (.609), slugging percentage (1.000), and he had 8 stolen bases, which set a playoff record. He easily picked up the series MVP.

Jose Canseco smashes his 31st homer of the year in 1988 during a game against the Chicago White Sox.

The A's were now headed for the first-ever, all-Northern California World Series. Oakland and the Giants of San Francisco were only separated by a bay.

Although the two cities were only a few miles apart, and the Athletics easily won in a four-game sweep, the Series still took more than two weeks to complete.

Prior to Game 3, as the two teams were warming up at San Francisco's Candlestick Park, the ground began to shake. A major earthquake, measuring 7.1 on the Richter Scale, caused massive damage and loss of life in both Oakland and San Francisco.

It caused some structural damage to the stadium but no one was injured on the field. The World Series was postponed for 11 days because of the earthquake.

The Athletics were the 1989 World Champions. Although they had one of the best baseball teams ever assembled, this Series will best be remembered for the break in-between.

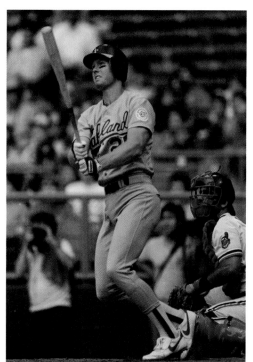

Mark McGwire watches his third home run of the day clear the outfield fence during a 1987 game against the Cleveland Indians.

The Best Talent Comes Up Short

In 1990, the pressure was again on the A's. With almost everyone back, the team would be very disappointed if it did not repeat.

The A's ran away with their third-straight AL West pennant. Then they clobbered the Red Sox in a four-game sweep to head back to the World Series, and hopefully win back-to-back titles.

The Cincinnati Reds had upset the heavily favored Pittsburgh Pirates in the NLCS to advance to the World Series. But most felt it would be down hill from there for the Reds. The A's were now being called a dynasty, and they would officially get that label as soon as they dismantled the NL champs.

The Reds stole Game 1 of the World Series and then never looked back, winning three more and sweeping the Series from the defending World Champions. In one of the greatest upsets in World Series history, the much more talented team lost—and lost badly.

Will They Recover?

The stunned A's never really recovered from the 1990 season. The following year they finished in fourth place. In 1992, they came back and won the AL West for the tenth time—the most of any major league team since divisional play began in 1969—only to lose to the Blue Jays in six games. In 1993, they fell to last place in the AL West—a place they hadn't been since the days of Charlie O.

The Athletics stayed in the AL West in 1994 when another division was added to each league. It didn't matter, because the season was canceled due to a players strike. The A's dropped to last again in 1995.

Changes are needed if the A's want to start winning again. So far, most of the changes have not been positive. In 1992, they traded slugger Jose Canseco. And recently they lost manger Tony LaRussa, who took them to three World Series. They also lost Rickey Henderson, Dennis Eckersley, and Danny Tartabull.

Although it doesn't look good for the Athletics, the franchise always manages to make it back. They have had some of the greatest teams in baseball history, and then have fallen off. They have also had some of the worst teams, only to come back and have a dynasty.

The team has moved from coast to coast, and had success on both sides of the country. They won with Connie Mack, who will never be forgotten, and they won with Charlie O. Finley, who can't be forgotten. They won with great teams, and they won with angry teams.

One thing is for certain, though. The A's, with their colorful roller coaster history, are bound to win again.

Glossary

All-Star: A player who is voted by fans as the best player at one position in a given year.

American League (AL): An association of baseball teams formed in 1900 which make up one-half of the major leagues.

American League Championship Series (ALCS): A best-of-seven-game playoff with the winner going to the World Series to face the National League Champions.

Batting Average: A baseball statistic calculated by dividing a batter's hits by the number of times at bat.

Earned Run Average (ERA): A baseball statistic which calculates the average number of runs a pitcher gives up per nine innings of work.

Fielding Average: A baseball statistic which calculates a fielder's success rate based on the number of chances the player has to record an out.

Hall of Fame: A memorial for the greatest baseball players of all time, located in Cooperstown, New York.

Home Run (HR): A play in baseball where a batter hits the ball over the outfield fence scoring everyone on base as well as the batter.

Major Leagues: The highest ranking associations of professional baseball teams in the world, currently consisting of the American and National Baseball Leagues.

Minor Leagues: A system of professional baseball leagues at levels below Major League Baseball.

National League (NL): An association of baseball teams formed in 1876 which make up one-half of the major leagues.

National League Championship Series (NLCS): A best-of-seven-game playoff with the winner going to the World Series to face the American League Champions.

Pennant: A flag which symbolizes the championship of a professional baseball league.

Pitcher: The player on a baseball team who throws the ball for the batter to hit. The pitcher stands on a mound and pitches the ball toward the strike zone area above the plate.

Plate: The place on a baseball field where a player stands to bat. It is used to determine the width of the strike zone. Forming the point of the diamond-shaped field, it is the final goal a base runner must reach to score a run.

RBI: A baseball statistic standing for *runs batted in.* Players receive an RBI for each run that scores on their hits.

Rookie: A first-year player, especially in a professional sport.

Slugging Percentage: A statistic which points out a player's ability to hit for extra bases by taking the number of total bases hit and dividing it by the number of at bats.

Stolen Base: A play in baseball when a base runner advances to the next base while the pitcher is delivering the pitch.

Strikeout: A play in baseball when a batter is called out for failing to put the ball in play after the pitcher has delivered three strikes.

Triple Crown: A rare accomplishment when a single player finishes a season leading their league in batting average, home runs, and RBIs. A pitcher can win a Triple Crown by leading the league in wins, ERA, and strikeouts.

Walk: A play in baseball when a batter receives four pitches out of the strike zone and is allowed to go to first base.

World Series: The championship of Major League Baseball played since 1903 between the pennant winners from the American and National Leagues.

Index